Oxford Read and Discover

Wild Ca

T0048902

Rob Sved

Contents

OXFORD
UNIVERSITY PRESS

OXFORD
UNIVERSITY PRESS

Great Clarendon Street, Oxford, OX2 6DP, United Kingdom

Oxford University Press is a department of the University of Oxford. It furthers the University's objective of excellence in research, scholarship, and education by publishing worldwide. Oxford is a registered trade mark of Oxford University Press in the UK and in certain other countries

First published in 2013

2018 2017 2016 2015 2014

10 9 8 7 6 5 4 3 2

ISBN: 978 0 19 464635 2

An Audio CD Pack containing this book and a CD is also available, ISBN: 978 0 19 464645 1

The CD has a choice of American and British English recordings of the complete text.

An accompanying Activity Book is also available, ISBN: 978 0 19 464656 7

Printed in China

This book is printed on paper from certified and well-managed sources

ACKNOWLEDGEMENTS

Illustrations by: Kelly Kennedy pp.11, 13; Alan Rowe pp.20, 21, 22, 23, 24, 25, 26, 27, 30, 31.

The Publishers would also like to thank the following for their kind permission to reproduce photographs and other copyright material: Alamy pp.3 (pet cat/Chris Howes/Wild Places Photography, tiger/Juniors Bildarchiv/GmbH), 8 (jaguar/Jeremy Graham), 15 (tiger/Juniors Bildarchiv/GmbH); Ardea.com pp.5 (black-footed cat Chris Harvey), 6 (cheetah family/Ferrero-Labat), 12 (M. Watson), 16 (Suzi Eszterhas), 17 (tiger cubs playing/M. Watson); Corbis pp.3 (lion/Hoberman Collection), 9 (lion/Hoberman Collection), 17 (cougar carrying young/Robert Lindholm/Visuals Unlimited), 19 (Pawel Libera); FLPA pp.4 (Gerard Lacz), 7 (sand cat/Gerard Lacz), 11 (ocelot/Rolf Nussbaumer/Imagebroker, lynx/Bernd Rohrschneider); Getty Images pp.5 (margay/Visuals Unlimited, Inc./Gregory Basco), 7 (mountain cat/Gunter Ziesler/Peter Arnold), 10 (Martin Harvey/Peter Arnold), 15 (leopard and snake/Per-Gunnar Ostby/Oxford Scientific); Naturepl.com pp.6 (tiger in grass/Sandesh Kadur), 8 (clouded leopard/Edwin Giesbers), 13 (Andy Rouse), 18 (Karl Ammann); Oxford University Press p.14; Science Photo Library p.9 (black leopard licking/Joe McDonald/Visuals Unlimited).

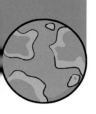

Introduction

Pet cats live with people. People give them food. Wild cats don't live with people. They live outside and they find food.

What cats can you see here?
What wild cats do you know?

Now read and discover more about wild cats!

Wild Cats

There are wild cats all around the world. Cats live in cold places and in hot places. Cats live on the ground and in trees.

The snow leopard is a big cat. It lives in snowy mountains. It has thick fur to stay warm.

A Snow Leopard

A Margay

The margay lives in rainforests. It can climb well, and it lives in trees.

The black-footed cat is a little cat. It lives in hot places. It can't climb well. It lives in holes in the ground.

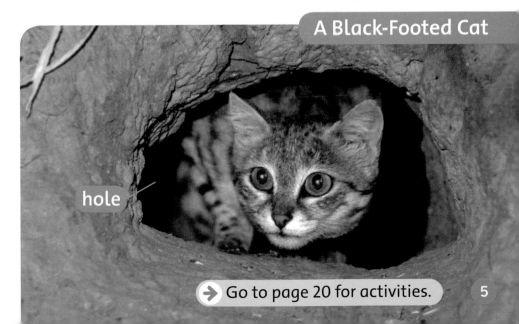

A Black-Footed Cat

hole

Go to page 20 for activities.

2 Fur

Cheetahs

spots

Cats have fur to stay warm. Their fur helps them to hide from other animals, too. Cheetahs have spots. Baby cheetahs have long white fur, too. They can hide in grass.

Can you see the tiger? Tigers have orange and black stripes. They can hide in long grass.

A Tiger

grass

stripes

rocks

A Mountain Cat

The mountain cat has spots and stripes. It can hide on rocks.

Discover!

Sand cats have fur on the bottom of their paws! This protects them from hot sand.

sand

paw

Go to page 21 for activities.

3 Mouths and Teeth

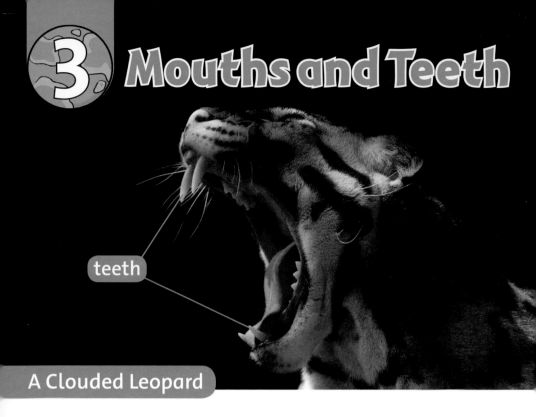

teeth

A Clouded Leopard

Cats have a big, strong mouth. They have long, sharp teeth, too. The clouded leopard has four long teeth to help it to hunt deer, monkeys, and birds.

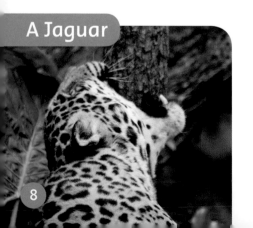

A Jaguar

Many cats bite trees. This makes their teeth very sharp. Look at this jaguar. Can you see its sharp teeth?

A Lion

Some big cats use their mouth to roar. Then other cats know where they are. They roar to say they are angry or sad, too. Lions can roar very well.

Discover!

Cats use their long tongue to clean their fur.

tongue

Go to page 22 for activities.

A Serval

Cats use their senses. They can hear, see, and smell very well. This helps them to move around and to hunt other animals.

The serval has big ears. It hunts mice. It can hear the mice under the ground.

An Ocelot

Cats can see well at night. The ocelot has white fur around its eyes. This helps it to see well.

Some cats can smell well, too.

Discover!

The lynx can smell a rabbit that's 300 meters away!

Go to page 23 for activities.

5 Tails

Many cats have a long, strong tail. Their tail helps them to run and turn. The puma uses its tail to help it to jump and land on its paws. Cats can use their tail to show they are happy, sad, or scared, too.

A Puma

tail

Snow Leopards

The snow leopard has a long, thick tail. It can put its tail around its body. This helps it to stay warm in the snowy mountains.

 Discover!

The jaguar uses its tail to hunt fish! It moves the water with its tail.

→ Go to page 24 for activities.

 # Food

Cats eat meat. Big cats hunt antelopes, zebras, and other big animals. They hide in grass and look for animals. Big cats are strong and they can run very fast to hunt other animals.

This cheetah sees an antelope. It runs fast to hunt the antelope.

cheetah

antelope

snake

A Leopard

Some cats eat birds, mice, and other little animals. This leopard eats snakes.

A Tiger

claw

Cats have long, sharp claws to help them to hunt other animals. Look at this tiger. It has very sharp claws!

→ Go to page 25 for activities.

7 Baby Cats

Cats protect their babies from other animals.

Baby cats can't eat meat. They drink milk from their mother. This mother lion has milk for two baby lions.

Lions

Cougars

Cats help their babies to move around. This mother cougar carries a baby in her mouth.

Baby cats love to have fun. They jump and play together. This is fun, and it helps the babies to learn how to hunt.

→ Go to page 26 for activities.

8 Protect Cats!

Many wild cats are in danger. Some people cut down trees in rainforests. Then some wild cats don't have a home or food.

Many big cats are in danger. Some people hunt big cats for their skin. Then they sell the skins.

Skins

Many zoos protect wild cats. They give the cats food and they help the cats to have babies. You can see lots of different wild cats in zoos. Wild cats are amazing. Protect wild cats!

A Zoo

→ Go to page 27 for activities.

① Wild Cats

← Read pages 4–5.

1 **Where do they live? Match. Then write the numbers.**

1 a black-footed cat

2 a margay

3 a snow leopard

in snowy mountains

in rainforests

in holes in the ground

 3

 ☐

 ☐

2 **Complete the sentences.**

hot ~~big~~ climb fur

1 The snow leopard is a ____big____ cat.

2 The black-footed cat lives in _____ places.

3 The snow leopard has thick _____.

4 The margay can _____ well.

② Fur

← Read pages 6–7.

1 Write the words.

> stripes ~~spots~~ grass rocks

1 <u>spots</u>   2 _____

3 _____   4 _____

2 Write *true* or *false*.

1 Mountain cats can hide on rocks.   <u>true</u>

2 Baby cheetahs have stripes.   _____

3 Tigers have orange and green stripes.   _____

4 Sand cats can walk on hot sand.   _____

3 Mouths and Teeth

← Read pages 8–9.

1 Find and write the words.

k	f	d	e	e	r
v	p	i	t	b	u
n	b	i	t	e	d
r	o	a	r	l	v
t	o	n	g	u	e
n	t	e	e	t	h

1 _deer_   2 _____

3 _____   4 _____   5 _____

2 Circle the correct words.

1 Cats have a (big) / little mouth.

2 Clouded leopards have six / four long teeth.

3 Many cats bite / eat trees.

4 Cats use their tree / tongue to clean their fur.

(4) Senses

← Read pages 10–11.

1 Write the words. Then match.

1 $rlse^av$

    <u>serval</u>

2 $n\lfloor xy$

    _____

3 lo_oc^te

    _____

4 cm^ei

    _____

2 Complete the sentences.

> fur   ears   smell

1 The serval has big _____ .

2 The lynx can _____ very well.

3 The ocelot has white _____ around its eyes.

5 Tails

← Read pages 12–13.

1 Write the words.

land   jump   run   turn

1 _____   3 _____

2 _____   4 _____

2 Write *true* or *false*.

1 All cats have a short tail.   _____

2 Cats use their tail to show they
   are happy.   _____

3 The snow leopard can use its tail
   to stay warm.   _____

4 The jaguar uses its ears to hunt fish.   _____

(6) Food

← Read pages 14–15.

1 Find and write the words.

antelope lionbirdsnakeclawszebra

1 _____ 2 antelope 3 _____

4 _____ 5 _____ 6 _____

2 Match.

1 Some cats eat

2 Big cats can run

3 The leopard

4 The tiger has

very fast.

eats snakes.

sharp claws.

antelopes and zebras.

7 Baby Cats

← Read pages 16–17.

1 Write the words.

milk   hunt   meat   mouth

1    **2**    **3**   **4**

1 _____   3 _____

2 _____   4 _____

2 Write the numbers.

1    **2**    **3**    **4**

1 The mother cougar carries her
   baby in her mouth.   3

2 Baby cats play together.

3 Baby cats drink milk from their mother.

4 A mother cat protects her babies.

8 Protect Cats!

← Read pages 18–19.

1 Write the words.

1 od°f

_____

2 l_sel

_____

3 oᶻo

_____

4 gₙaᵉdr

_____

5 ikˢn

_____

6 ʳfstaⁱnᵒer

_____

2 Match.

1 Some people cut down	protect animals.
2 Some people hunt big cats	trees in rainforests.
3 Some zoos	for their skin.

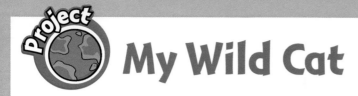

My Wild Cat

1 Choose a wild cat. Write its name. Draw and color your cat.

Name: _____

2 **Write the words.**

tail   fur   legs   paws   claws
teeth   eyes   ears   mouth   nose

3 Write about your wild cat.

What is it?

_____

Is it big or little?

_____

Is its tail short or long?

_____

What color is it?

_____

Where does it live?

_____

What does it eat?

_____

What can it do?

_____

_____

_____

Picture Dictionary

 bite

 clean

 climb

 cut down

 danger

 deer

 food

 fur

 ground

 hide

 hunt

 land

 meat

 mice

 mountain

 night

paw

people

pet cats

protect

rainforest

roar

sell

sharp

smell

strong

tail

thick

turn

warm

wild cats

world

Oxford Read and Discover

Series Editor: Hazel Geatches • CLIL Adviser: John Clegg

Oxford Read and Discover graded readers are at six levels, for students from age 6 and older. They cover many topics within three subject areas, and support English across the curriculum, or Content and Language Integrated Learning (CLIL).

Available for each reader:
• Audio CD Pack (book & audio CD)
• Activity Book

Teaching notes & CLIL guidance: www.oup.com/elt/teacher/readanddiscover

Subject Area / Level	The World of Science & Technology	The Natural World	The World of Arts & Social Studies
1 — 300 headwords	• Eyes • Fruit • Trees • Wheels	• At the Beach • In the Sky • Wild Cats • Young Animals	• Art • Schools
2 — 450 headwords	• Electricity • Plastic • Sunny and Rainy • Your Body	• Camouflage • Earth • Farms • In the Mountains	• Cities • Jobs
3 — 600 headwords	• How We Make Products • Sound and Music • Super Structures • Your Five Senses	• Amazing Minibeasts • Animals in the Air • Life in Rainforests • Wonderful Water	• Festivals Around the World • Free Time Around the World
4 — 750 headwords	• All About Plants • How to Stay Healthy • Machines Then and Now • Why We Recycle	• All About Desert Life • All About Ocean Life • Animals at Night • Incredible Earth	• Animals in Art • Wonders of the Past
5 — 900 headwords	• Materials to Products • Medicine Then and Now • Transportation Then and Now • Wild Weather	• All About Islands • Animal Life Cycles • Exploring Our World • Great Migrations	• Homes Around the World • Our World in Art
6 — 1,050 headwords	• Cells and Microbes • Clothes Then and Now • Incredible Energy • Your Amazing Body	• All About Space • Caring for Our Planet • Earth Then and Now • Wonderful Ecosystems	• Food Around the World • Helping Around the World